EXTRAORDINARY ANIMALS

CALCULATING CHIMPANZEES, BRAINY BEES,

AND OTHER ANIMALS WITH

MIND-BLOWING MATHEMATICAL ABILITIES

Stephanie Gibeault

illustrations by Jaclyn Sinquett

mit Kids Press

For Dr. Suzanne MacDonald,
who encouraged my love of animal cognition
SG

For Foo, best friend to critters everywhere
JS

• • •

Text copyright © 2024 by Stephanie Gibeault
Illustrations copyright © 2024 by Jaclyn Sinquett
Cover illustrations copyright © 2024 by Jaclyn Sinquett
Cover photographs: copyright © 2024 by Sandris Veveris/Shutterstock (bee, purple flower);
Russell Watkins/Shutterstock (chimpanzee); Courtesy of Dr. Sarah Benson-Amram (hyenas);
Astrid Gast/Shutterstock (bee, yellow flower); slowmotiongli/Shutterstock (shoal of guppies);
Fedor Selivanov/Shutterstock (parrot)

Additional image credits appear on page 82.

The MIT Press, the ≡mit Kids Press colophon, and MIT Kids Press are trademarks of The MIT Press,
a department of the Massachusetts Institute of Technology, and used under license from The MIT Press.
The colophon and MIT Kids Press are registered in the US Patent and Trademark Office.

First edition 2024

Library of Congress Catalog Card Number pending
ISBN 978-1-5362-3001-7

24 25 26 27 28 29 CCP 10 9 8 7 6 5 4 3 2 1

Printed in Shenzhen, Guangdong, China

This book was typeset in Amasis MT Pro.
The illustrations were created digitally.

MIT Kids Press
an imprint of Candlewick Press
99 Dover Street
Somerville, Massachusetts 02144

mitkidspress.com
candlewick.com

CONTENTS

INTRODUCTION

HAVE YOU HEARD the story about the world's smartest animal? In the early 1900s, a horse named Hans answered questions. Not just your average questions—but challenging math problems! What if your pets were that smart? Your dog could help with math homework by barking correct answers. *Woof!* Or your cat by swishing her tail. Seems too good to be true, right? Yet every day, crowds in Germany gathered to see Hans, Wilhelm von Osten's brainy horse, answer math problems.

Von Osten was a retired schoolteacher. He spent years treating Hans like one of his students. Except instead of giving grades, he would reward the horse with bread and carrots. Von Osten taught Hans colors, the alphabet, and how to tell time. And, of course, he taught him math.

Von Osten wanted people to see what Hans could do. So, he and his horse put on shows for the public. Von Osten would ask the audience for questions. Then Hans would tap out the answer with his hoof. Sometimes the questions

CLEVER HANS HAS A LESSON WITH VON OSTEN.

involved counting, like how many women in the crowd were wearing a hat. Other questions asked Hans to add or subtract two numbers. He was even asked questions with fractions. For example, $\frac{2}{5} + \frac{1}{2}$. Hans would tap his answers, first the numerator, then the denominator, and was almost always correct. Wunderbar!

Newspapers nicknamed the horse Clever Hans, and he and von Osten became worldwide sensations. Even the *New York Times* declared: "BERLIN'S WONDERFUL HORSE; He Can Do Almost Everything but Talk." Although many experts trusted the horse's abilities, not everybody believed in Clever Hans. A psychologist named Oskar Pfungst was certain there was more to the story. He decided to test Hans.

Pfungst knew that if Hans were really solving problems, he would tap correctly even if nobody else knew the answer ahead of time. So, Pfungst designed an experiment where only the horse knew the entire question. Pfungst would whisper a number in Hans's ear so quietly that no one else could hear it. Next, von Osten, the horse's owner, would do the same with another number. Then, Hans was asked to add the two numbers together. Nobody knew the answer until Hans finished tapping. Finally, Pfungst and von Osten said their numbers out loud. They repeated this test thirty-one times. Hans was right only three times. Then they repeated the experiment. But this time the men told Hans their numbers out loud so everybody could hear them. Hans was right twenty-nine out of thirty-one times. There was the catch. For Hans to tap correctly, the people around him needed to know the answer first.

Was Hans reading people's minds? Of course not! He wasn't doing calculations, either. Pfungst realized von Osten was the one doing the math. Hans simply tapped his hoof until he saw von Osten signal him to stop. But it was not a trick. Von Osten didn't know he was signaling the horse. Without realizing, he would move his head slightly when Hans reached the correct number of taps. When Hans saw this tiny movement, he would put his hoof back on the ground.

All those years of schooling had not taught the horse math. They had taught him how to read a person's body language. No matter who asked the question, Hans could read their movement. Hans was certainly clever—just not in the way his fans and the newspapers had thought.

After learning about Clever Hans, you probably have doubts about any animal doing math. It's just too complicated, right? Surely only humans can understand numbers. Many people used to agree. Number skills were once believed to be uniquely human and beyond the brainpower of any other creature. Now we know that's simply not true.

For years, scientists have studied what animals know about numbers. But after Clever Hans, scientists have been more careful about how they ask their questions. They don't want to be fooled again. Instead, they design controlled experiments to reveal how animals think. Scientists make sure not to give any clues about the correct answer. And guess what? They have discovered that even though Clever Hans couldn't do math, other animals can.

Some animals have mind-boggling number skills. We know that fish can tell large numbers from small ones. Hyenas count. African grey parrots use symbols to represent numbers. Chimpanzees do addition. And honeybees understand zero. Amazing! How do they do it, and why have they developed these skills? Read on to discover all about the mathematical abilities of animals.

CHAPTER 1
FISH FIGURES

GUPPIES are tiny fish with tiny brains—more than one thousand times smaller than your brain. But could Gloria the guppy secretly be a math genius? Well, maybe don't hire her as your math tutor, but she likely has some impressive number skills. You see, guppies like to hang out in a group of fish called a shoal. You might have thought it was called a school—and you'd be close. A school is a shoal of fish all swimming in the same direction. When given a choice, guppies prefer larger shoals to smaller ones. Larger shoals provide more protection from predators. It's a matter of life and death! So, guppies should be able to tell large groups from small ones.

How does a guppy decide which shoal to swim in? If one shoal has four guppies and another shoal has two, would she know? And would she have to count to figure it out? Counting might seem like the most basic math skill. But there is another, simpler skill the guppy could be using. And you use it, too.

IT'S A MATTER OF LIFE AND DEATH!

Have you ever divided a group of people into teams? Sometimes teams are almost equal in number, say eight players to nine. At a glance, the teams look about the same size. So, you have to count to see if they are equal. After all, you don't want one team to have an unfair advantage. But sometimes, two teams are far from equal. Maybe there are ten on one side and two on the other. Then it's easy to tell that one team has more players. You don't have to count. You can eyeball the teams and know they're different. Scientists call this a **RELATIVE NUMEROSITY JUDGMENT**. You don't have to know the exact number on each team to judge their relationship to each other.

This ability to naturally understand quantities is called your number sense. It's shared by all humans, even babies. Many animals have a number sense, too, from mammals to birds to insects. What about guppies? Do they share our knack for numerosity? Dr. Christian Agrillo, an associate professor of psychology at the University of Padova in Italy, wanted to know. His field of research includes studying the numerical abilities of fish. He figured that if guppies prefer larger shoals, they can probably eyeball numbers the same way we can. So, he and his team did an experiment to test whether guppies can make relative numerosity judgments.

Dr. Agrillo's team needed only three fish tanks and some guppies to carry out their experiments. They placed a single guppy in one fish tank, called the subject tank. At one end of the subject tank, they placed another tank containing a large shoal of guppies. At the opposite end of the subject tank, they placed a third tank with a small shoal of guppies. Then the scientists watched to see where the single guppy swam inside the subject tank. Did it swim to the

RELATIVE NUMEROSITY JUDGMENT: Numerosity *refers to the number of items in a group.* And relative judgment *means comparing the two groups and deciding which one has more items than the other.*

GUPPY GOSSIP

Guppies are also known by the scientific name *Poecilia reticulata*. They are small tropical fish common in aquariums all over the world. Silver-gray females can grow up to 2 $\frac{2}{5}$ inches (6 centimeters) long. Males are about half that size. They liven up a fish tank because the colorful males sport stripes, spots, or shiny iridescence. In nature, guppies are usually duller in color than those bred in captivity for aquariums. They are found naturally in northeastern South America and the nearby islands of the eastern Caribbean, although people have introduced them to bodies of water all over the world. Some of these guppy habitats are full of hungry predators like wolffish and cichlids. How do the tiny guppies avoid being lunch? They live in shoals.

Swimming in shoals protects a guppy in many ways. One is simply a matter of the odds. The more fish a predator has to choose from, the less chance of any one fish being the snack. That's the eat-my-buddy-instead-of-me strategy. A large group may also confuse predators. It makes it harder for them to pick out an individual target. Plus, a fish swimming alone has to keep a lookout ahead, behind, above, and below. But a fish swimming in a shoal has a whole group of eyes searching for potential danger. It's no wonder guppies like to hang out with their friends. And it's no wonder they've developed the ability to compare group sizes and choose to join the larger shoal. It helps them survive!

A COLORFUL MALE GUPPY

end of the tank beside the smaller shoal or to the end beside the larger one? The scientists repeated the experiment again and again with different test guppies swimming alone in the tank.

And wait! There was one more part to the experiment. Think like a scientist. Remember how Clever Hans watched his owner for clues? What else could the test guppies notice about the shoals besides number? Do larger shoals take up more space? More fish look like a thicker blob and fill more of the tank. Could patterns and shapes guide the fish's preference? A shoal of three might look like a triangle, and a shoal of four like a square. Does color impact their choice? More guppies might be shinier or brighter. Or is there some other quality we can't even imagine because we don't have fish brains?

To stop the guppies from using the clues above, the scientists placed dividers in the tanks. First, there were dividers in the end tanks to separate each member of a shoal into its own area. That stopped the shoal members from swimming in a group. Next, there were dividers in the subject tank to block the test guppies' view of the end tanks. Now the test guppies could see only one fish in each shoal at a time. They had to swim around the subject tank to see all the other guppies before choosing a side. They couldn't use the thickness, pattern, shape, or color of the shoals. That forced them to use numerosity when making their choice. And guess what? They swam near the larger shoal!

So, guppies have a number sense, too. But is it like ours? Scientists think there may be two number systems working in the human brain that help us with numbers. One is called the **OBJECT-TRACKING SYSTEM**. It's an exact system, but it has a limit. It works only for small numbers—one through four.

OBJECT-TRACKING SYSTEM: *a number system that lets you track up to four objects separately*

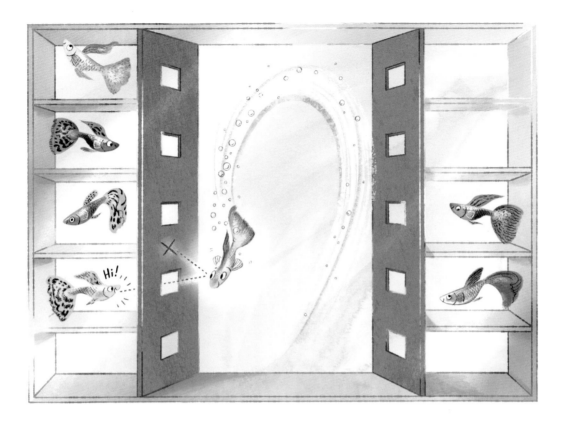

The second system is called the **APPROXIMATE NUMBER SYSTEM**. This system has no limits. But it makes estimates rather than tracking each object. Because this system is based on estimates, it's not always consistently accurate. The accuracy in telling two groups of objects apart is affected by the size of the groups and the difference between them.

First, consider the size of the groups. It's easier to tell the difference between smaller groups. For example, a plate of four chocolate chip cookies is only one larger than a plate of three. But it's obvious they're not the same. It's harder when you look at larger groups. Think about two baking sheets covered in freshly baked cookies. A difference of

APPROXIMATE NUMBER SYSTEM: *a number system that lets you estimate an unlimited number of objects*

THANKS TO THE NUMERICAL SIZE EFFECT, IT'S EASY TO TELL THE DIFFERENCE BETWEEN THESE TWO PLATES OF COOKIES BECAUSE THERE IS SUCH A SMALL NUMBER OF COOKIES ON EACH PLATE.

only one cookie can be incredibly difficult to see. You would have to count to tell which sheet has the most cookies. This is known as the **NUMERICAL SIZE EFFECT**.

Second, consider the difference between groups. The smaller the difference, the harder it is to tell them apart. One chocolate chip cookie versus twenty is an obvious difference. No counting required. Nineteen cookies versus twenty is much harder to judge. Nobody will notice a cookie missing from that baking sheet. Yum! This is known as the **NUMERICAL DISTANCE EFFECT**.

Remember, the numerical size effect and the numerical distance effect come into play only with the approximate number system. If you're using your object-tracking system, you will be just as accurate no matter what the group sizes are, as long as they're four or under. It's thought that animals share the

THANKS TO THE NUMERICAL DISTANCE EFFECT, IT'S TRICKY TO TELL THE DIFFERENCE BETWEEN THESE TWO BAKING SHEETS. BECAUSE THEY ARE ONLY ONE NUMBER APART ON THE NUMBER LINE, YOU NEED TO COUNT THE COOKIES.

approximate number system. But do they share the object-tracking system? To answer this question, Dr. Agrillo designed an experiment that compared guppies to university students.

Let's go back to the three tanks from the earlier experiment, but this time there aren't any dividers. A single test guppy was again put in the center subject tank, and the scientists repeated the experiment again and again with different test guppies. Then the scientists watched to see how long the test guppies swam near the larger shoal or the smaller shoal in the end tanks. The test guppies saw ten different combinations of shoals, from one guppy in one end tank versus four in the other, to four in one versus sixteen in the other.

When the test guppies chose between shoals of four or fewer fish, they spent more time swimming beside the larger shoal, no matter what the shoal sizes were. The test guppies found it just as easy choosing a shoal of four fish over one as choosing a shoal of two over one. The size of the difference between the two shoals didn't seem to matter. That sounds a lot like the object-tracking system.

When the test guppies chose between shoals of four or more fish, the difference in number between the two shoals became important. The more similar the shoals were in number, the harder it was for the fish to tell them apart and swim beside the larger shoal. They couldn't accurately tell them apart. For example, telling four guppies from six guppies was harder than telling four from sixteen. Sounds like the approximate number system.

Don't forget that Dr. Agrillo's team tested university students, too. They showed them the exact same pattern that they showed the guppies, but the students didn't swim around in a giant fish tank! They sat in front of computer screens and looked at two groups of dots and, unlike the fish, were instructed to find the larger group as fast as possible. When the screen showed four or fewer dots, the difference didn't matter. The students were quite accurate and fast. But when the groups of dots were larger than four, it was more difficult to tell the difference. The closer the numerical distance, the longer it took to choose and the more the students' accuracy dropped.

Was Dr. Agrillo's team surprised by these results? Not for the people. They expected the students to perform differently with groups of four and under versus groups larger than four. That's thought to be the switching point between the object-tracking system and the approximate number system. The surprise was the guppies. They showed the same switching point. Do they have an object-tracking system, too? Dr. Agrillo thinks they might. It's exciting to think that guppies and people might have so much in common. But more research needs to be done.

HOW TO DESIGN
A NUMBER EXPERIMENT

When scientists do number experiments with animals like guppies, they can't give them instructions about what to do. So, they have two choices: they can look at the animals' natural behavior, or they can train them. With natural behavior, scientists offer a choice of appealing items and see which one spontaneously attracts the animal. They might present two pieces of food on one side of the test area and three pieces on the other. A lot of animals will prefer to go to the three pieces so they can eat more. Because they choose the larger pile, the scientists can assume the animals can tell the two amounts apart. But it's hard to control variables in these experiments. Variables are the factors that influence the animal. For example, three bananas could have more yellow than two bananas. So, the animal might choose based on color rather than number. On the other hand, if you train an animal, you can carry out more complicated experiments that control the variables. For example, you can train an animal to touch dots on a computer screen. Once they understand the rule, such as "touch the larger number," you can test their numerical abilities. But training takes time and is harder to do with animals in the wild.

THREE BANANAS HAVE MORE YELLOW THAN TWO BANANAS.

SUMMING IT UP

I had the chance to interview **DR. AGRILLO** in May 2022 about his guppy research. Here's what he had to say.

Q: Why did you choose to study fish?

A: There are not a lot of experiments done on numerical abilities in fish. We wanted to study an animal that was not already well studied. But we also wanted to understand the very origins of numerical abilities in humans and animals. Fish split off from land vertebrates, like reptiles and mammals, approximately 450 million years ago. If you find a similarity in the way fish and humans think, especially in numerical abilities, that means those abilities might have evolved early in evolution.

Q: When you repeated the guppy experiment with humans, did you tell the humans what to do even though you couldn't tell the fish?

A: In some studies, in the very beginning, we gave the people instructions. But later, we stopped doing that. When we compare humans to monkeys or fish, humans are in front of a computer screen. They have to touch a button to start, try different things, then find the rule, like touch the larger group of dots. My experience is that after four or five trials humans find the rule because very often it's easy. They see a large group of dots and they see a small group of dots. They try choosing one of the groups by chance, then another, and then they get the point. That makes it fair because that's the way the animals have to find the rule.

Q: What stopped the people from counting the dots instead of just doing what the guppies were doing?

A: It's not the way you study at school. It's not one plus one plus one. If it was, humans would choose correctly 100 percent of the time in these experiments. It would be simple arithmetic. Instead, if you present the dots quickly—for instance, 150 milliseconds—humans cannot easily count each dot. With a fast presentation, people estimate. For thousands of years, humans had to solve these types of problems, like figuring out which is the larger group of friends or food. And that is the skill we want to compare with animals rather than the symbolic numerical abilities you learn in school.

Q: How can guppies have a similar number sense to humans when they have such small brains?

A: This is an open debate in comparative psychology right now. Some years ago, we assumed the larger the brain, the better. And there is still a positive correlation, of course. The more the brain weighs in comparison to the rest of the body, the higher the cognitive skill or the smarter the animal probably is. But now some people believe it's not about size or the number of neurons in the brain, but a question of the complexity of the interaction between those neurons. If you have one million neurons but there are few connections, your brain might not work as well. If you have only one thousand neurons but those neurons have a lot of interconnections, it could increase your ability to solve tasks. For instance, bees have an even smaller brain compared to fish. But they likely have very complex cognitive skills.

ACTIVITY
KNOW YOUR NUMEROSITIES

Try testing your number sense with some relative numerosity judgments. That means comparing two groups of objects and knowing which is bigger. Remember, no counting!

YOU'LL NEED:

- a partner
- forty identical objects, like dimes or candies
- a cell phone or stopwatch
- pencil and paper

1. Have your partner sit at a table with their eyes closed.

2. Set up two groups of objects on the table in front of your partner—one smaller than the other. You don't need to use all the objects. Write down the number of objects in each group and the difference between them on the paper.

3. Be ready to start the timer on the phone or stopwatch as soon as your partner opens their eyes.

4. Tell your partner to open their eyes and point to the larger group as fast as they can (without counting).

5. Write down the time it took for your partner to choose—and whether they were correct.

6. Repeat steps one through five, but change the number of items in each group. Again, write down the results.

7. Keep repeating the experiment with different-sized groups. Try small groups like two and three. Try large groups like nineteen and twenty. Try large differences between groups like two and twenty. Or small differences like fifteen and sixteen. What do you notice in your partner's results? When was their fastest time? When was their slowest? Were they more accurate with small numbers or with larger ones? How did the difference between groups affect their accuracy and speed?

8. Switch places with your partner and repeat the entire experiment. What did you notice?

Try placing the objects in patterns, like rows of five or triangles. Does that help your accuracy and speed? What if the objects are spread out instead of close together?

CHAPTER 2
COUNTING CALLS

HYENAS TALLY INTRUDERS

SPOTTED HYENAS (*Crocuta crocuta*) live in Africa south of the Sahara Desert. Although they have a reputation as scavengers, they are one of the top predators on the continent. Adults have powerful jaws and weigh up to 190 pounds (86 kilograms). Hyenas live in clans—groups of up to ninety hyenas. Each clan defends a territory against other hyena clans. And fights between clans can be deadly. When clashes happen, the larger group usually wins.

But the whole clan doesn't hang out together all the time. Instead, small groups or single hyenas spend much of their time traveling, looking for food, or resting. What does one hyena or a small group do if they encounter hyenas from another clan? Without the support of the rest of their clan, they are at risk of injury or death. Defending the territory is important, but they need to judge whether it's safe to attack. It's too dangerous to fight if there are more intruders than hyenas on the home team. The odds are in the intruders' favor.

If there are more home-team hyenas than intruders, it's safer to approach and run them off. The odds are in the home team's favor.

Do hyenas know the odds? And if so, how? Do they count the number of intruders and compare it to the number of home-team hyenas? That's probably what you would do. Counting involves knowing the exact number of items in a group, like the number of hyenas in a clan. It also means knowing that five hyenas equal the same number as five cookies. It doesn't matter what you're counting—five is five, three is three, and so on.

Wait a minute. You can tell that there are three cookies on a plate without counting them, right? True! For small numbers, you can know the exact amount without counting. That's called **SUBITIZING**. The word *subitizing* comes from the Latin word for *suddenly*, because that's how it works. *Boom!* There are two dots on that domino. *Boom!* You rolled a four on that die. You just know, quickly and without effort, how many objects there are. Scientists think this ability is thanks to the object-tracking system mentioned in chapter 1. It even works with touch and sound as well. As long as the numbers

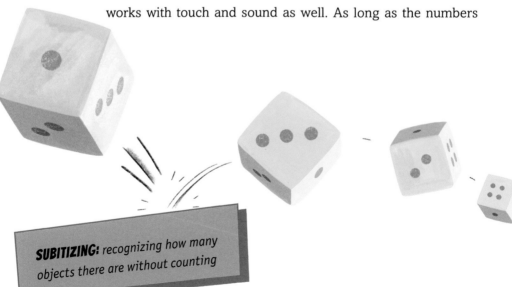

SUBITIZING: recognizing how many objects there are without counting

are low, you can know how many cars honk in a traffic jam or the number of times an adult calls you for dinner just by subitizing.

Whether hyenas count or subitize, Dr. Sarah Benson-Amram wanted to know if they calculate the odds when they encounter intruders. Dr. Benson-Amram, a behavioral and cognitive ecologist at the University of British Columbia in Canada, studies carnivore behavior. To test the hyenas, she and her fellow scientists performed a sneaky experiment. No, they didn't dress up like intruding hyenas. They played recordings of hyena calls to fool hyenas into thinking there were intruders nearby. They used this trick on spotted hyenas living in the Masai Mara National Reserve in Kenya. That's a 580-square-mile (1,510-square-kilometer) nature park that is also home to lions, leopards, and black rhinos. Researchers have been watching these hyenas for thirty years, so the presence of humans doesn't bother the animals.

All Dr. Benson-Amram needed were recordings of hyenas from unfamiliar clans making a call known as a whoop. Both males and females of all ages whoop to stay in touch over long distances. And every hyena's whoop

THE HYPE ABOUT HYENAS

Spotted hyenas are named for their coarse, spotted coats. In fact, each hyena has a unique pattern of spots that helps researchers tell them apart. You might think they look like wild dogs, but they are more closely related to cats. Because of the giggling sound they make, they are also known as the laughing hyena. But hyenas don't tell jokes. They giggle when they're stressed. Hyenas also use many other calls, including the whoop, that can be heard from three miles (five kilometers) away.

Females are in charge of hyena clans—every female is the boss of every adult male. Plus, the group has a **LINEAR DOMINANCE HIERARCHY**. Higher-ranking animals

A HYENA RESTS IN THE GRASS.

have first access to food. Clan members spend a lot of time alone or in small groups, especially during the day. They rejoin the clan at kills or to defend their territory. After all, there is strength in numbers when you're chasing lions away from your dinner. Hyenas will also gather at the den, which is where they raise their young. This system of splitting apart and rejoining is known as a **FISSION-FUSION SOCIETY**.

HYENAS DON'T TELL JOKES. THEY GIGGLE WHEN THEY'RE STRESSED.

is slightly different. So, hyenas can tell one another apart by their voices. If a whoop comes from a clan member, they might go over to the whooper or whoop back. But a whoop from an unknown hyena, like those used by Dr. Benson-Amram, means an intruder is in the territory.

Whoops were played through a hidden speaker mounted on the scientists' research vehicle. Then the scientists videotaped different test hyenas to see what they would do when they heard the sounds. Sometimes the test hyenas were alone, and sometimes they were in small groups. After hearing the sounds, the test hyenas could act aggressively and approach the speaker to take on the intruders. Or they could be careful and avoid the speaker, perhaps retreating or whooping to their clan members for reinforcement.

RESEARCHERS OBSERVE A SPOTTED HYENA FROM THEIR TRUCK.

Hyenas whoop in bouts that average around six whoops per bout. All the test hyenas heard three whoop bouts in a row, so eighteen total whoops. Sometimes there were three whoop bouts from the same intruder. Sometimes it was one intruder making two whoop bouts and another intruder making one whoop bout. And sometimes there were three different intruders whooping. Because each test hyena heard the same number of whoops, they couldn't decide what to do based solely on the number of whoops they heard. Instead, they had to judge whether they heard one, two, or three different intruders. Plus, the whoops were played one at a time. The hyenas had to keep track in their memory. The question was, Would the test hyenas play the odds? For example, if they heard three different whoopers while they were alone, would they retreat? And would they approach if they heard two different whoopers while they were in a group of three? In other words, would they count the number of intruders and compare it to the number of clan members in their own group?

FROG LOVE SONGS

Other animals besides hyenas can tally sounds, including frogs and toads. Together, frogs and toads are known as anurans. Many male anurans have an interesting way of attracting a female. They make special calls to advertise their presence and convince the female they are the best choice of partner. How does a female decide which male has the best call? In some species, it's all about how many notes the male sings. The one who sings the highest number of notes will win the female's attention. So, males try to one-up one another, adding note after note in a sort of singing competition. If frog A sings two notes, frog B will sing three, and so on. In other species of anurans, males use these call competitions to threaten one another. Why don't the males just make as many notes as possible every time? Because it's exhausting. Instead, they make only as many notes as they need to. And it's likely they do it by tracking the exact number of notes other males are making.

That's exactly what the test hyenas did! The more intruders they heard, the more attention they paid to the sounds, sitting up and turning their heads. And when their group outnumbered the intruders, they were more likely to take a risk and aggressively approach the speaker, searching the area to find their rivals. Remember, the hyenas didn't see the intruders to make a relative numerosity judgment, like the guppies did. Because they didn't hear all the whoops at the same time, they had to remember each intruder's whoop and tally the total number of whoopers.

Before you whoop it up, know that some scientists would say the hyenas can't be counting, at least not the way we do. They would call it a counting-like ability, or proto-counting. You probably count without any difficulty. So, it's tempting to think, *What's the big deal?* But how exactly do you count? Try it right now by counting the number of words in this sentence. What did you do? You used number words as labels, either out loud or in your head. The label *one* meant you saw one word, the label *two* meant you saw a second word, and so on until you reached the word *thirteen*.

It's unlikely hyenas have number words. They howl, wail, whoop, and laugh, but they don't have humanlike language. So, they can't be counting like people do. At least not the way we count when we have number words. (Not all human cultures do.) However, the test hyenas tallied the intruders. They compared the number of whoopers they heard with the fellow clan members they saw and knew the difference. They could have been subitizing to make

WHAT DOES IT MEAN TO COUNT?

Counting with number words has many parts. You understand that each item you're counting has a unique number label, and you don't count the same item twice. That's known as one-to-one correspondence. You also put the number labels in proper order. *Two* always comes before *three* and after *one*, for example. That's known as the stable order principle. Additionally, you understand that the final label you say represents the total number of items you counted. That's called cardinality.

their decision. After all, the numbers were low. But it's likely they were counting in their own hyena way. Unfortunately, Dr. Benson-Amram's team simply didn't gather enough data to know for sure. Either way, the hyenas seemed to know the exact number of intruders and home-team friends. These spotted predators are smarter than most people think.

A HYENA WATCHES THE RESEARCH TRUCK.

SUMMING IT UP

I was able to interview **DR. BENSON-AMRAM** about her hyena research in July 2022, and here is what she told me.

Q: During your playback experiment, how did you fool the hyenas into believing other hyenas were around?

A: I parked the car a bit far away from a resting hyena or a group of hyenas. Then I waited until they stopped looking at me and returned to what they were doing before I arrived. Next, I placed the speaker facing out the window away from the hyenas so it would sound like the calls were coming from behind the car. In a few of the trials, the hyenas would run over to try to find the intruders. They would usually run past the car, then start sniffing around and looking. We also only did a few trials per individual hyena, and we made sure to space the trials out over a few weeks so the hyenas wouldn't learn that the calls weren't from real animals.

Q: How did the test hyenas know they were hearing different hyenas whooping rather than just one hyena whooping many times?

A: Our experiment showed that hyenas can tell one another apart by their voices, just like we can. When I hear hyenas whooping, I can tell some of them apart and some of them sound more similar to me. The same thing happens in people. Some people's voices sound really different, and some people, like two brothers or two sisters, may sound similar and harder to tell apart unless you really know them. I think the same is true for hyenas. You can also look at the structure of the whoops by making a picture of the sound, called a spectrogram. When you do that, you can also see and measure the differences between the calls from different hyenas.

Q: Did hearing the pretend intruders' whoops scare the test hyenas?

A: As scientists, we can document and measure an animal's behavior, but we can't know for sure how that animal is feeling—for example, whether they are anxious and scared. Some hyenas in our experiment would pop their head up, listen to some of the calls, and then just go right back to sleep. So, they were probably not feeling very worried or scared. Other hyenas would listen carefully for a long time. Still others would run toward the speaker. Those hyenas may have been feeling more scared, or perhaps angry. We can't be sure. However, if they did feel these emotions, I don't think they felt them for very long. Once the calls stopped and/or they searched the area and did not find any intruders, they tended to go back to what they were doing before. Also, we did not see any big, long-lasting changes in their behavior after the experiment.

Q: How do hyenas act when they meet real intruding hyenas?

A: Hyenas react very similarly to real-world intruders as they do to pretend intruders. Their behavior depends on the situation. For example, if they are alone, they tend to be more cautious. If they are in a group, they tend to be more aggressive. They also will call for help. They whoop and other hyenas from their clan come over to help. We see this both when hyenas are faced with intruders and also when they come across lions, particularly if there is food involved.

Hyenas can tell individual voices apart and subitize or count what they hear. Can you do the same?

YOU'LL NEED:

- a partner
- a cell phone to record and play sounds
- at least four other people who you can record
- paper and pencil

1. Record yourself and your partner making a whoop sound. Then record four other people's whoops until you have recorded six different whoops.

2. With your partner, listen to all the whoops and divide them equally into two teams: the home team and the intruders. On the paper, list the names of the people on each team. Include yourself on the home team.

3. Give your partner the paper, and send them into the next room.

4. Have your partner make a list on the paper of the recordings they will play. They can choose the number of whoops and the order. For example, they might play three home-team whoops, then two intruder whoops, then one more home-team whoop. They don't have to use all the recordings. They can even use the same person's whoop multiple times.

5. Now your partner should play the whoop recordings one at a time following their list. Count how many different home-team whoopers you think you hear compared to how many different intruders. Listen carefully. Can you tell the whoopers apart? Were there more intruders or more home-team members?

6. Using your partner's list, compare what you heard with what was played. Were you correct? Could you tell the whoopers apart? Was one team bigger than the other?

7. Switch places with your partner and play a different set of whoops for them. See who is better at tracking whoopers.

BONUS

Try recording a different sound, like the word *hi* or a grunt. Do different sounds make it easier or harder to tell people apart? Were you able to count them accurately?

CHAPTER 3

BIRD BRAINS

AFRICAN GREY PARROTS (*Psittacus erithacus*) are the largest of all the African parrot species. They live in flocks mostly in rain forests and are considered one of the smartest animals, right up there with dolphins and apes. Why are they so brainy? Well, African greys need a lot of brainpower just to survive in the wild. They have a lot to remember, like which plants are safe to eat. They also need to know how to avoid predators and defend their territory. Plus, they need to remember which trees have food and which ones they have already emptied. But most importantly, they need to keep track of all those fellow flock members.

The most famous African grey of all time was Alex. He lived in the United States in the lab of Dr. Irene Pepperberg, a comparative psychologist and president of The Alex Foundation. Years ago, Dr. Pepperberg decided to prove birds were smarter than many people thought. So, she went to a pet store to purchase an African grey. She asked the clerk to pick her parrot so nobody could later accuse her of selecting the smartest one. She named the parrot Alex, which was short for Avian Learning Experiment.

Alex loved bossing around the humans in the lab and playing with corks, cardboard boxes, and key chains. He also liked coaching the other birds who joined him later. Unfortunately, Alex passed away at the age of thirty-one, which is young for an African grey. He had hardened arteries, the blood vessels that carry blood from the heart to the rest of the body, and he died suddenly without suffering. Through all their experiments, Alex and Dr. Pepperberg changed the scientific community's opinion of what birds can do.

Because parrots can imitate human speech, when Dr. Pepperberg and her team asked Alex questions, he could answer with words of his own. First, she taught him label words, starting with *paper* because he liked to chew it. To teach him, Dr. Pepperberg and another trainer would ask each other about a paper object while Alex watched. They would identify it as *paper*, then exchange the object. Next, they would ask Alex what the object was. If he said *paper*, he would get the object to chew on. But he wasn't just mimicking the sounds the trainers were making. Within a few weeks, Alex asked for a piece of paper all on his own to wipe some apple off his beak. This was a breakthrough! He understood what *paper* meant and used the label appropriately. After working with Dr. Pepperberg for over thirty years, Alex knew more than one hundred spoken labels. When he saw a painted wooden shape, he could answer "What color?" "What shape?" or "What matter (material)?" If he was shown a metal key and a plastic key, he could answer "What's different?" or "What's same?"

What is a label exactly? It's a symbol that represents something real. Think about sheet music. The notes on the page are symbols that represent certain sounds. The notes don't make music—the musician playing them does. When it comes to quantities, we have two kinds of symbolic labels: number words and Arabic numerals. Number words are *one, two, three,* and so on. Arabic numerals are symbols like 1, 2, and 3. When you first learned to count, you needed to understand that the numeral 4 meant four items. You also had to

PARROT PRATTLE

African grey parrots are believed to be the bird best at imitating human speech. They use their voices to communicate with other parrots in the wild. They have even been known to imitate other animals. So, when they live with people, it's only natural they will imitate to try to fit into their human flock. This skill makes them popular pets. However, keeping an African grey is a huge responsibility. They require loads of attention and mental exercise. Plus, they have long life spans of over fifty years. Due to logging and the illegal trapping of wild parrots for the pet trade, they are endangered. Even parrots bred in captivity often come from wild-caught parents. If you insist on having an African grey as a pet, it's essential to only purchase from a reputable breeder. Or even better, adopt one in need of a new home.

These birds are incredibly social. Before wild populations were devastated by trapping for the pet trade, African greys roosted overnight in massive flocks that could include over one thousand members. During the day, they would separate into much smaller groups of around thirty birds. Today, the flocks include around one hundred birds and the smaller groups around a dozen. The daytime groups fly long distances looking for food. Most of what they eat is found in trees and includes fruits, nuts, and seeds. Members of a flock talk to one another with loud and noisy calls. They use these sounds to organize their movements and warn one another of danger. Birds might also squawk as they compete for the best nesting spots—holes in trees.

A FLOCK OF AFRICAN GREY PARROTS LAND ON THE GROUND.

learn that the word *four* meant four items. And finally, as a result, the number 4 and the word *four* represented the same thing. That's known as **EQUIVALENCE**. Your teacher can ask you "What is four plus four?" Or she can write "4 + 4 = ?" Both have the same meaning.

Symbolic labels don't match the things they represent. The symbol is random! For example, the shape of the number 8 doesn't look like eight objects. It looks like a little snowman. So, you can't automatically understand number labels by their shapes or sounds. You have to memorize them. Because Alex had done so well with his colors and shapes, Dr. Pepperberg wanted to teach him symbolic number labels.

First, she taught him the number words from one to eight. To test his understanding, a researcher would show him a tray covered in different objects, like wooden popsicle sticks and pennies. Then the researcher would

EQUIVALENCE: *The idea that number words, numerals, and items in a group can all be swapped for one another. They're equal.*

ask Alex something like "How many wood?" Alex had to ignore the pennies and just count the popsicle sticks. He was very good at this. Researchers also showed him a tray with different-colored objects. There might be six blue blocks, five red blocks, and four green blocks. When they asked Alex "What color four?" he was able to tell them green. He could even do this with objects he had never seen before.

ALEX COUNTS THE NUMBER OF GREEN BLOCKS ON THE TRAY.

To make sure she had enough data, Dr. Pepperberg's team would ask Alex these questions over and over again. But Alex would get tired of answering. When he'd had enough, he would act like a naughty child. Sometimes he would refuse to answer. Sometimes he would lift his butt toward Dr. Pepperberg. And once he grabbed the tray in his beak and flung it to the floor before saying "Wanna go back."

But there was still so much to learn about bird brains. So, Dr. Pepperberg also taught Alex Arabic numerals, starting with 1 to 6, by matching them with their number words. He knew the numeral 4 was the same as the spoken word *four.* But Dr. Pepperberg was careful to never show Alex the numeral 4 paired with four items. She wanted to see if Alex could make the connection all by himself using equivalence. For example, if he truly understood that the numeral 2 was the same as the word *two,* he would also know that the numeral 2 represented two physical objects. The label words could connect the two concepts.

In addition, Dr. Pepperberg wondered if Alex understood, without any training, that 2 is smaller than 3 but greater than 1. That's called **ORDINALITY**. It answers the question "What position?" It's more than memorizing the labels. It's understanding their place (their order) on the number line.

Dr. Pepperberg designed an experiment to test Alex's understanding of equivalence and ordinality. This was a tall order. Remember, Alex had never learned to match Arabic numerals with numbers of objects. He also learned his number words out of order. Dr. Pepperberg first taught him the labels *three* and *four.* That was based on the shapes he'd learned earlier—a triangle was "three-corner" and a square was "four-corner." Next came *two* and *five.* They were one more and one less than what he already knew. Then he learned *six.*

SOMETIMES HE WOULD LIFT HIS BUTT TOWARD DR. PEPPERBERG.

ORDINALITY: *the sequencing of numbers in the correct order*

One was the last label she taught him. Until then, he had always been able to get a single object by saying its label. For example, he could get a popsicle stick by saying "wood." Now having to say "one wood" confused him. It took him over a year to get it. All of this was different from how children learn their numbers. You were probably taught from smallest to largest. So, Alex had a bigger challenge!

To test Alex, Dr. Pepperberg's team placed two Arabic numerals that were two different colors on a tray: for example, a red 2 and a yellow 4. Then a researcher would ask Alex which color was bigger or smaller. If Alex answered by saying the wrong color, the researcher removed the tray, turned away from him, and said "No!" Then the researcher would turn back and ask him again. If he answered by saying the correct color, the researcher praised him and gave him the number as a toy to chew on. Incredibly, Alex was right almost every time without any specific training.

Another test involved putting one Arabic numeral on a tray beside a group of objects, such as wooden blocks. The numeral and the objects would be two different colors and two different equivalencies—for example, a blue number

TRAINING A SOCIAL BIRD

Dr. Pepperberg set out to prove the limits of bird intelligence. She didn't want to watch parrots in the wild; she wanted to communicate with them directly and discover how much they could learn. To do that, she used a technique that was groundbreaking at the time. Because of Clever Hans, scientists were convinced they couldn't interact with the animals they were studying. The risk of influencing the animal's behavior was considered too great. But Dr. Pepperberg realized that a social animal would likely learn best in a social way. She believed she couldn't study communication in parrots without actually communicating with one.

Dr. Pepperberg used a training technique known as the model/rival program. Two trainers would work together to show Alex what they wanted him to do. The first trainer would ask the second trainer to name an object with its label word. If the second trainer answered correctly, she got the object as a reward. If she answered wrong, she was told a harsh "No." In this way, the second trainer modeled the behavior Dr. Pepperberg wanted Alex to learn and also acted as a rival for Dr. Pepperberg's attention.

Alex watched the two trainers interact, taking turns being the model. Then one of the trainers would turn to Alex and ask him the same question. The hope was that he would learn from observation and answer correctly for a chance to play with the object. And that's exactly what he did. This social bird bonded with his trainers and especially with Dr. Pepperberg, and he learned all the better for it.

5 would be placed beside four yellow blocks. Again, Alex was asked "What color bigger?" or "What color smaller?" This could have easily confused him. Four wooden blocks are physically bigger than a small plastic numeral. They take up more space on the tray. Alex could have answered about the physically

bigger or physically smaller object. But this super-smart parrot used ordinality and chose the correct number almost every time.

How did Alex do it? It looks like he did it the same way we do—by using equivalence. He understood that random symbols like words or numerals represent real things. Then, by comparing what the symbols represented, he could choose the larger or smaller number based on ordinality. And most amazingly, he said his answer out loud. Looks like it's not so bad to be called a birdbrain after all!

Does this experiment remind you of anything? How about Clever Hans from the introduction? Just as von Osten asked his horse questions, Dr. Pepperberg and her team asked Alex. But Dr. Pepperberg knew the risk of giving the parrot cues. She used plenty of inventive controls to make sure no one could tell Alex the right answers, even by accident. For example, the person asking the questions wasn't the person scoring the answers as right or wrong. A second researcher, who didn't know what was on the tray, marked down the words Alex said. Also, the researchers who had taught Alex his number and color labels had worked with him years earlier. If he had learned cues from them, they were no longer around to give them. Plus, Alex was saying labels, not tapping until he saw a cue to stop. No horsing around in that lab.

SUMMING IT UP

I interviewed **DR. PEPPERBERG** in May 2022 about her research with Alex. Here's what I learned.

Q: What was Alex's favorite thing to say?

A: That changed all the time. He did seem to enjoy playing with the sounds of his words and trying to make up new ones. Because if he came up with an actual new word, we quickly gave him some new item that matched the label! So, for example, once he learned "gray" by asking "What color?" to his image in a mirror. Then he said "grape," "grain," "chain," and "cane." He immediately got the fruit, some interesting seeds, a paper-clip chain, and some sugarcane.

Q: Why did you reward Alex with the objects he had labeled instead of with food?

A: We wanted him to understand the direct connection between the object he was identifying and the label he was producing. We started training him with objects that he really enjoyed chewing apart so he would be eager to learn the label in order to get the object to chew. If we had given him food rewards, he would have thought that all his labels simply meant "feed me." Plus, we didn't want to restrict his diet in any way because we thought that would simply make him cranky and stupid. How would you feel if you didn't have lunch and then someone was making you answer a bunch of questions to get fed?

Q: Did Alex enjoy the number experiments?

A: I don't think he enjoyed number studies at first because he didn't care to receive several of the objects—which were his reward. A single piece of wood was interesting, but many were boring. So, we trained him to say, "I want *blank*." Then he could toss the object he had identified if he didn't like it and ask for what he wanted. Once he could do that, he became more interested.

Q: When Alex said the wrong answer, did it bother him when you told him "No!"?

A: Probably, but sometimes he gave wrong answers when he was bored. He seemed to enjoy seeing his trainers get more and more frustrated. We knew he probably didn't understand why he had to identify the same thing over and over. But we needed to show that he could do it often enough that it wasn't just chance. When he was "acting up," it was very clear. He would give us all the possible wrong answers, one by one, carefully avoiding the correct response. He couldn't do that just by chance!

ACTIVITY
SYMBOL SKILLS

Make up your own number symbols. They can be shapes, squiggles, or even upside-down letters. Then try teaching a partner your new numerals without saying a word.

YOU'LL NEED:
- a partner
- pencil and paper
- nine slips of paper
- nine identical objects, like dimes or candies

1. Design your own number symbols for the numbers 1 to 9 on the paper. Then make a chart matching each number to its symbol.

2. Once you're happy with your symbols, draw each one on its own slip of paper.

3. Place one of your symbol slips in front of your partner. Then place the matching number of objects beside it. Tell your partner that these are number symbols and that they should try to memorize them for a math problem later.

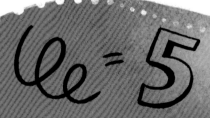

4. Remove the first symbol slip and the objects, then place a different symbol slip in front of your partner. Again, place the matching number of objects beside the slip.

5. Repeat with all your symbol slips until your partner has seen every one paired with the matching number of objects.

6. Write a math problem on another piece of paper (for example, 4 + 3 = ?), but substitute your symbols for the numbers. Give the problem to your partner. Did they understand your symbols well enough to solve it?

7. Have your partner make up a new set of number symbols and repeat the activity. Can you solve their math equation?

BONUS

Create a symbol for 10. You can use a zero symbol and add it to your 1 symbol. Or you can make an entirely new symbol. What would you do for 15 or 20?

CHAPTER 4
APE ADDITION

CHIMPANZEES (*Pan troglodytes*) are famous for their intelligence. They have a complex culture in the wild, and in captivity they have been taught to use American Sign Language. You might think chimpanzees are monkeys, but just like gorillas, orangutans, bonobos, and humans, they are actually great apes. In fact, chimpanzees are humans' closest living relative. You share over 98 percent of your DNA with a chimpanzee. That's thanks to a common ancestor who lived at least six million years ago.

Found in central and western Africa, chimpanzees are an endangered species due to habitat loss and hunting. Their diet includes leaves, bark, flowers, insects, and even animals like monkeys. To make life easier, chimpanzees use tools to capture their meals. They collect insects and grubs with sticks. They use stones to smash open nuts. And they even sop up water with sponges made of leaves. They love ripe fruit, too. But they need to decide which trees to feast in. Instead of wasting their efforts on a small amount of food in a nearby tree, they need to calculate if it's worth traveling to a faraway tree that's bursting with fruit. Will the energy they gain from the more fruitful tree make up for the energy they use getting there?

CHIMPANZEE CHATTER

Chimpanzees live in fission-fusion societies where members come and go depending on what's happening. Their life can be stressful. These territorial animals will fight with neighboring groups. In fact, researchers have seen chimpanzee groups go to war, deliberately killing other chimpanzees to take over their territory. Life inside the group can be tense at times, too. Males have a strict dominance hierarchy with an alpha male in charge of the whole group. Females have a hierarchy, too, although the alpha female usually ranks lower than the alpha male.

ONE CHIMPANZEE GROOMS ANOTHER TO MAINTAIN THEIR ALLIANCE.

Higher-ranked chimpanzees have better access to resources like food. Because of this pecking order, chimpanzees spend a great deal of time worrying about climbing the social ladder. They will often form partnerships with others in the group by grooming or sharing food. These alliances can be used to raise their status or even overthrow the alpha. All this scheming might also explain chimpanzees' math skills. They need to know how many friends they have before starting a fight, whether it's within their group or with the group next door.

You might expect such clever creatures to possess mathematical abilities. And they do. Chimpanzees can make relative numerosity judgments, count, and use symbols like Arabic numerals. What else can they do? What about performing arithmetic? Can you teach addition to a chimpanzee? Or do they already know how to do it on their own? In a way, counting objects one at a time is a form of addition. For each new object counted, you just add one to the total. For simple addition, you don't even need symbols or formulas. Number labels are not required. Believe it or not, human babies can actually do simple addition.

You can show a baby a toy, then hide that toy behind a screen. Next show the baby another toy. Hide it behind the screen. Amazingly, the baby knows there should be two toys behind the screen now. If you secretly place a third toy behind the screen without the baby noticing, the baby will stare in surprise when you lift the screen. The baby expected to see two objects but instead saw three. The same thing happens if you secretly take one toy away. So, even though babies don't have number labels, the baby must be adding and subtracting.

That's something you would expect all kinds of animals to be able to do, too. If a squirrel sees two cats slink under a shrub, he will wait for two cats to come back out before collecting his acorns. But unlike squirrels, babies soon become toddlers and start learning number words and Arabic numerals. That eventually leads to calculations using those symbolic labels, such as the equation $2 + 3 = 5$. If chimpanzees understand Arabic numerals, can they add with them, too? It's time to meet Sheba the chimpanzee.

Sheba was raised in a human home until she was two and a half years old. Then she moved to a lab at The Ohio State University in the United States, where she lived with two other chimpanzees, Darrell and Kermit. They were all participating in Dr. Sarah Boysen's research. Dr. Boysen is a retired comparative psychologist who studied chimpanzee and capuchin monkey cognition, which means the way they think. Because chimpanzees are highly social, Dr. Boysen could work with them all day just like a teacher with children in preschool—teaching lessons and playing games such as chase and tickling. Dr. Boysen and her team were able to teach Sheba all kinds of things, including sorting colors, sorting shapes, and drawing.

SHEBA HANGS OUT IN THE LAB, GROOMS DR. BOYSEN, AND COMPLETES A NUMBER EXPERIMENT.

Dr. Boysen wanted to look at Sheba's number sense, too. Starting when Sheba was four years old, Dr. Boysen taught her to recognize and use Arabic numerals. (Although chimpanzees can understand spoken language, they are unable to make human speech sounds. So, Dr. Boysen couldn't teach Sheba to say number words.) Dr. Boysen showed Sheba groups of gumdrops or other treats and asked her to choose the matching Arabic numeral. If Sheba chose wrong, Dr. Boysen put a new arrangement of gumdrops and numerals in front of her and asked her to choose again. But if Sheba chose right, she got to eat the treats. Delicious! Dr. Boysen taught Sheba each numeral one at a time, and Sheba had to choose correctly 90 percent of the time before the next numeral was introduced. This gradual progress helped Sheba learn such a complex concept more easily. By the time she was five, Sheba knew her numbers up to eight.

Now it was time for a completely new task. Dr. Boysen wanted to see if Sheba could add groups of objects. Three places in Sheba's classroom were chosen as hiding spots: a tree stump, a food bin, and a plastic dishpan. A table across the room held cards labeled with the numerals 1 to 4. Between one and three oranges were hidden in two of the three hiding spots for each trial. Dr. Boysen hoped Sheba would explore the room, find the two groups of oranges, and return to the table leaving the oranges in their hiding spots. Then Sheba could point to the number that showed how many oranges she had seen.

Dr. Boysen thought Sheba would need help understanding what to do. So, for the first few trials, she took Sheba by the hand and walked her around the area, pointing out the oranges and saying, "Sheba, look there!"

IF SHEBA CHOSE RIGHT, SHE GOT TO EAT THE TREATS. DELICIOUS!

Once they had gone by all three sites, she took her over to the work area where number cards were laid out. Dr. Boysen asked Sheba, "How many oranges did you see?" Sheba figured it out right from the first trial! Apparently, she didn't need help after all. She couldn't see all the oranges at once. And she couldn't see any oranges when she was sitting at the number table. Yet she chose the correct number for the sum of all the oranges right from the start. That's incredible! That meant she understood how many oranges were in each group. Then she combined those numbers and picked the label that represented the total.

To make the problem even harder, Dr. Boysen took the oranges away. She replaced them with cards showing Arabic numerals, from 0 to 4. Now when Sheba searched the hiding spots, she found numbers instead of food. For example, there might be a 2 in the tree stump and a 1 in the food bin. Again, Sheba had to visit all the hiding spots, then return to the table and choose the number that equaled the total. You might think the new rules bewildered

THE LABORATORY VERSUS THE WILD

When studying animals, scientists can either work in the animals' home environment or bring the animals into a human one such as a laboratory. Doing research in the wild allows you to see a creature's natural behavior—what they do on a day-to-day basis. Also, you are less likely to influence animals, especially if you keep out of sight or get them used to your presence first. That's like Dr. Benson-Amram's hyena study. Researchers had been watching those hyenas for so long that they weren't affected by the trucks and people. When Dr. Benson-Amram played the whoop calls, the hyenas believed they were coming from other hyenas rather than from the humans.

But working in the wild can be challenging. You can't control whether the animals want to participate in your experiment, and you can't control all the variables or factors that affect their performance. For example, it would be impossible to control the size of shoals if you studied guppies in a river. The more variables you can control, the more you can pinpoint the reason for an animal's actions. So, working with captive animals allows for more complex and precise experiments. Plus, you can discover an animal's full potential. Chimpanzees don't use Arabic numerals in the wild, but Dr. Boysen revealed they can do it when given the chance.

Life in the lab, however, can influence an animal's behavior. For instance, if food and shelter are provided, the animal doesn't have to spend the day searching for them. They might spend more time resting than they would in the wild. It's also essential that scientists consider a captive animal's well-being. All the animal's physical, emotional, and psychological needs should be met, and that's an incredibly challenging thing to do. Finally, just because one or two animals can do something in the lab, it doesn't mean the entire species would express that behavior in their natural habitat.

What do you think is the better approach? Would you rather sit in a forest or wetland and devise clever ways to test wild animals? Or would you rather control all the variables but risk affecting the animal's natural behavior? It all depends on the question you're asking and the animal you're studying.

Sheba. But she immediately switched to numerals in her mind. In her first session of twelve trials, she was right ten times. Wow, so smart!

Dr. Boysen made sure she didn't accidentally help Sheba the way von Osten helped Clever Hans. For the oranges experiment, Dr. Boysen sat at the table with her back to the food sites. Then for the Arabic numeral experiment, she sat behind Sheba. That meant Sheba couldn't see Dr. Boysen, and Dr. Boysen couldn't see the number Sheba chose. It was only after Sheba held her finger on a number card that Dr. Boysen came around and looked at her choice. This meant Dr. Boysen didn't influence Sheba or give the right answer away by mistake.

Without any earlier addition training, Sheba used some kind of process to add. But nobody knows exactly what. We know she wasn't subitizing, because she couldn't see all the oranges at once. But she might have been keeping a running total. That's known as **COUNTING ALL**. Or perhaps she used **COUNTING ON**. So, if there were two oranges in the first hiding spot, she would start counting from three at the next hiding spot.

Either way, Sheba summed the Arabic numerals as successfully as she did the oranges. The symbols didn't confuse her at all. She knew a 2 represented two oranges, so she could use the same addition process whether it was fruit or number cards. Did you notice the number zero was included in the second experiment? And even in the first experiment with the oranges, an empty hiding spot was sort of like zero as well. That didn't throw off her addition, either. Impressive, right?

COUNTING ON: *starting your count with the total of the first group, then adding one for each item from there*

COUNTING ALL: *starting at one and adding one for each item until you get to the last item*

SUMMING IT UP

In May 2022, I interviewed **DR. BOYSEN** about her research with Sheba. This is what she told me.

Q: Were you surprised by the results of the oranges experiment?

A: I absolutely did not teach Sheba to "add" or "sum" foods, objects, or anything. She seemed to understand the game immediately and answered correctly for about 87 percent of the trials we ran. We were shocked that chimps are apparently able to come up with ways to add items. That's similar to the addition skills of young children around the age of three. It was very, very exciting! The same thing happened when I put out the Arabic numerals instead of the oranges. Sheba already knew "the game" and immediately switched in her mind to adding the symbols instead of counting oranges. I knew this was unprecedented in the animal literature and that a true breakthrough had occurred.

Q: Why did you choose Sheba for this experiment?

A: Sheba was still small enough to run free outside the cage without it being dangerous for me or her. Also, she and I were very, very close, like mother and daughter. So, I knew she would enjoy that task and I thought she trusted me enough to help her learn it eventually. Surprise, she already knew how to do this!

Q: How did you reward Sheba for a right answer? Did she eat the oranges?

A: No. The oranges were obvious to the eye, but she didn't really like them unless there was nothing else to eat! That's why I used them for the experiment. When she was correct, she got the matching number of gumdrops to eat. If the number was zero, though, she got a hug. I didn't confuse her by giving her a number of candies.

Q: Could Sheba subtract as well?

A: Yes, and it showed up exactly the same way as summation. The first time I tried to test her for subtraction, she got it right!

ACTIVITY
ADD IT UP

Put yourself in Sheba's shoes with this addition activity. Total the number of hidden objects but give the experiment a twist to up the challenge.

YOU'LL NEED:

- a partner
- at least ten of one type of object and ten of another, like ten candies and ten tennis balls
- four hiding spots
- pencil and paper
- calculator or phone app

1. Choose the first object, object A. Make it worth three of the other object, object B. For example, one candy could equal three tennis balls. So, if you saw one candy and two tennis balls, that would total the value of five tennis balls.

2. With your partner, choose four spots where you can hide objects.

3. Close your eyes. Then have your partner hide a random number of both object A and object B in at least three of the spots.

4. Open your eyes and visit all four hiding spots as fast as you can. Remember, object A counts as three object Bs. In your head, add the total number of object Bs. So, if you saw three candies (object A) and four tennis balls (object B), that would total the value of thirteen tennis balls.

5. Head to home base and write your answer down on the piece of paper. Now return to all the hiding spots and check your addition with a calculator. How did you do? Were you able to add all those numbers in your head? Did you do it with "counting all" or "counting on"?

6. Take turns with your partner and see who can add the most accurately.

BONUS Try making object A worth a different number of object B and repeat the activity.

1 candy
=
3 tennis balls

CHAPTER 5

INSECT INTEGERS

HONEYBEES UNDERSTAND ZERO

HONEYBEES (*Apis mellifera*) are tiny insects with huge importance for humans. We rely on them for honey and beeswax. But more importantly, they pollinate our fruits, vegetables, and grains. Without honeybees, we would struggle to produce enough food. But what do bees eat? They eat pollen and nectar from flowers. To make it easy to find the right flowers, honeybee workers communicate with one another by dancing. After finding food, a worker bee will return to the colony and perform the waggle dance. The dance communicates where the food source is, including distance, direction, and angle to the sun. After watching, the other workers can leave the hive and visit the same flowers. Isn't that amazing?

It seems this small insect with an even tinier brain is surprisingly smart. But what about math skills? Well, think about the waggle dance. It prevents other bees from wasting time and energy visiting empty flowers. And an empty flower represents nothing, which is similar to the mathematical concept of zero.

THE BUZZ ABOUT BEES

Honeybees are eusocial. That means the colony (all the bees who live together) functions almost like a single being. In eusocial animal societies, several generations live together at once. The colony also practices cooperative care of the young. Finally, they divide the necessary chores. These chores are done by different castes or groups. The three castes in a honeybee colony are the drones, the queen, and the workers.

The one hundred to five hundred male drones mate with the queen. The lone queen lays eggs that become baby bees. Then there are the workers. These are the other female bees, and there are up to fifty thousand of them! They take care of the young even though they aren't their own. They keep the hive in tip-top shape, defend it, and collect the food.

Worker bees need to remember which flowers they already emptied of pollen and nectar so they don't waste time with repeat visits. They also need to know how far they have flown and at what angle to the sun. Bees have even been shown to count landmarks. With such complex food-collecting behavior, maybe it's not so surprising they understand zero.

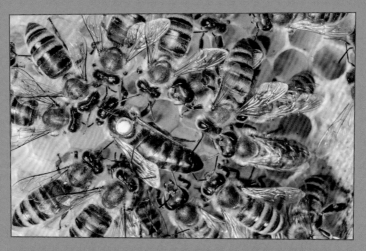

HONEYBEES IN A HIVE. THE QUEEN IS MARKED WITH A DOT.

Zero is a special number. After all, you couldn't do math without it. For example, you know 100 is different from 1 only because of those handy zeros. They act as placeholders in the ones and tens columns. Plus, zero sits at the middle of the number line. Positive **INTEGERS** go to the right of zero. And negative integers go to the left. So, is zero harder to understand than 1, 16, or 42? Absolutely!

You can't see zero and you can't count it. That makes it unlike any other positive number. Scientists believe there are four steps to understanding zero.

THE HISTORY OF ZERO

Surprisingly, humans had symbolic numbers long before they had zero. The ancient Romans used a number system with Roman numerals, where V equals 5 and X equals 10, for example. They had a sophisticated society with books, roads, and even underground sewers and public toilets. But they didn't have zero! In fact, zero came along pretty late in human culture.

A zero-like concept was first invented around 400 BCE. The Babylonians, who lived in what is now the area around Iraq, used wedge-shaped symbols for numbers. They had a special double wedge as a placeholder to indicate an empty column. Fast-forward four hundred years to the other side of the world in what is now Guatemala. There, the ancient Mayans used a shell-like symbol in the same way. However, these different symbols weren't yet considered numbers.

It wasn't until the year 628 CE that zero emerged as a number. That's when a mathematician in India provided rules for including zero in calculations. It was around six hundred years later, in 1200 CE, when an Italian mathematician finally introduced Arabic numerals, including zero, to Europe. In time, that system traveled around the world.

First, you must understand that it's the absence of something. For example, an empty glass. There's nothing inside for your eyes to see. Second, you need to realize that nothing is a meaningful category. You can compare nothing to something. Like a light being on versus a light being off. Third, you grasp that zero has a numerical value. It sits at the low end of the positive number line. So, just as 1 is less than 2, 0 is less than 1. And finally, you understand the numerical symbol 0 and can use it in calculations like $4 - 4 = 0$.

If it's so hard for people, what about for animals? Can they make sense of zero? Those little buzzing honeybees can—or at least the first three steps of understanding zero. It took humans hundreds and hundreds of years to include the concept in our mathematics, but in a number experiment, bees figured it out in a single day!

Dr. Scarlett Howard is a biologist at Monash University in Australia. She studies the way bees and other insects think. She was curious about whether bees could understand the idea of nothing and where it sits on the number line. So, Dr. Howard and her team taught a group of honeybees the concept of "less than." Their hives of bees were outside, so the bees were free to search for food where they pleased. But because they got sugar water for participating, they chose to visit Dr. Howard's experiments.

To test the bees' ability to learn "less than," the scientists used white cards with one to four black shapes printed on them. Each card had a small platform in front for the bee to land on. And each platform held a drop of liquid. If the bees chose one of the cards with the smaller number of shapes, the "less than" value, they found a drop of sugar water. Bees love sugar water. If the bees chose the larger number, the "greater than" value, they found a drop of quinine. Yuck! That's a bitter liquid that bees don't like drinking. Four cards were hung on a screen at a time, two correct and two incorrect. So, there might have been two cards containing four squares and two cards containing two squares for one trial. For another trial, there might have been three squares and two squares.

It didn't take the bees long to learn to choose the card with fewer shapes. Then it was time to test if they really understood "less than." Dr. Howard showed the bees cards with new shapes they hadn't seen before. So now instead of seeing squares, they would see circles. They still picked the smaller number. Next, she added zero and five to the mix. How did Dr. Howard show the bees zero? With a blank white card, of course. And amazingly, the bees chose the blank card. That showed they understood a blank card represented a lower number than a card containing shapes.

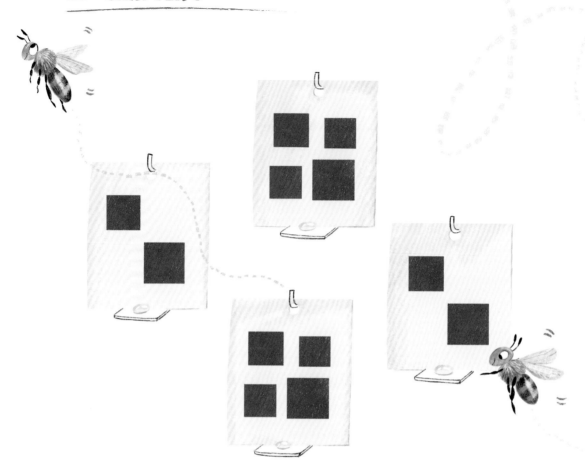

But Dr. Howard wanted to dig deeper. She wanted to look at the third stage of zero—recognizing zero's place on the number line. In studies of zero with people and monkeys, scientists noticed the numerical distance effect. Remember that from the guppy chapter? The larger the difference between two numbers, the easier it is to tell them apart. That means zero should be confused with the number one more than with two, three, or any other higher number. If the bees showed that trend, it would be proof of a mental number line.

So, Dr. Howard trained different bees to pick the smaller number using cards with zero to six shapes. The bees could tell all the numbers apart, including zero. And most importantly, they showed the numerical distance effect. They had an easier time with zero versus five and zero versus six than with zero versus one. Just like monkeys. And just like people. It seems that bees, with their teeny little brains, are much smarter than we think. Un-bee-lievable!

There are many possible reasons why honeybees need to do number tasks in the wild. First, it helps them compete with bees from other hives for access to flowers. If there are too many other bees near a patch of flowers, the bee knows to look somewhere else for food. Second, bees count landmarks to help them find their way to and from the hive. That delicious patch of clover might

A BEE DRINKS SUGAR WATER AFTER CHOOSING THE BLANK CARD THAT REPRESENTS ZERO.

ZERO MEANS NO COMPETITORS.

be three trees away, not two. Finally, bees might need to compare the number of flowers in different places. Why waste your time in a small patch of flowers when there is a bigger patch across the field? In all these cases, understanding zero could be helpful. Zero means no competitors. It also means you haven't hit the first landmark. And a flower you already emptied has zero food.

At what age do humans understand zero? You already know from the chimpanzee chapter that babies can solve basic addition problems. But those babies sure don't understand zero. It's not until children are about four years old that they can start to do what the bees can do. And of course, it's not until around five or six years old that children grasp the symbolic representation of zero: 0 or the word *zero*. After that, calculations with zero (step four) aren't too far down the road.

A HONEYBEE IN A FLOWERING LAVENDER FIELD

SUMMING IT UP

I had the opportunity to interview **DR. HOWARD** in May 2022 about her bee research, and here's what she had to say.

Q: How did you train the bees to leave their hive and participate in your experiment?

A: We brought a single bee to our experiment area on a spoon, which had a drop of sugar water on it. We then showed the bee that if she participated in experiments, she would get more sugar water. This single bee flew to her hive when she was full of sugar and then decided to come back to our experiment to learn and collect more sugar water. She made trips from her hive to our experiment many times throughout the day.

Q: How did you tell the bees in your experiment apart?

A: We put a small colored dot on the bees using a paint pen. Each bee had a different color and pattern so that we could easily tell them apart. The paint is usually used by beekeepers to mark queen bees in the hive. It doesn't harm the bees we work with.

Q: How many times have you been stung by the bees you work with?

A: I have not been stung many times. We usually only get stung when we are not cautious enough around bees. Honeybees are quite gentle and fun to work with—you just need to be careful with them.

Q: How do you know the bees don't like the bitter liquid you gave them if they chose wrong?

A: We know that bees love sweet things. The bitter liquid is far from sweet. If you don't believe me, you can watch a bee try to take a drink of the bitter liquid, spit it out, and fly away from it.

Q: How does your research help people?

A: It is important to understand the animals that we share our world with. Insects can often be forgotten because they are small and many people are afraid of them. When we learn that bees are necessary to grow food and that they are smarter than we thought, people better understand them.

ACTIVITY
BEE A SCIENTIST

Dr. Howard's team created an experiment that suited honeybees. But what about testing a different animal's understanding of zero? Pretend you're a scientist and try this thought experiment. Design a way to test any animal you like, from dolphins to butterflies.

YOU'LL NEED:
- paper and pencil
- books or access to the internet

1. Choose the animal you would like to test.

2. Research your chosen animal's diet and behavior using books or the internet.

3. Decide what you will use to represent numbers. Make it appropriate for your animal. For example, some monkeys eat fruit, so you might design a test that uses bananas attached to fake branches.

4. Choose a reward for your animal that suits their natural diet. A whale might like krill. An eagle might like fish.

5. Draw your experimental design on the paper. For example, will you use an aquarium with cards at either end? Then you could reward a dolphin if they swam to the right card. Will you use fake flowers with different numbers of petals? Then you could reward a butterfly if they landed on the right one.

6. Decide which number combinations you will use to teach your animal. Remember, you want them to learn to choose the lower number before you introduce zero. What will you use to represent zero? An empty branch? A flower without petals? When you introduce zero, what would you expect the animal to do? Why might your animal understand zero? Why might they not?

BONUS

How would choosing a different animal change your experimental design?

CONCLUSION

WOW! Animals have some amazing mathematical abilities. And what you learned in the previous chapters is far from the whole story. Did you know guppies also have a simple understanding of ordinality? Alex the African grey parrot could add. And chimpanzees grasp some of the concepts of zero. And those genius honeybees? Dr. Howard discovered they can tell the difference between odd and even numbers!

Other animals have shown talent with numbers as well—from tiny creatures like ants to humongous elephants. But what about poor Clever Hans? You might wonder if horses are the exception. Interestingly, scientists haven't studied them much. But horses seem to have a number sense, too.

In one experiment, scientists showed apples to horses. Then the scientists placed the apples in two buckets. The horses were free to choose one of the buckets by touching it with their nose. When the numerosities were small, the horses had no problem picking the bucket with more apples. And that makes sense. Horses love apples. Why wouldn't they choose more of them? But when the buckets held four and six apples, the horses picked at random. There's that magic number four again. Sounds a bit like the guppies.

Nobody has asked horses to add fractions since Clever Hans. And none of the animals tested so far have been doing the sort of mathematics humans can do. Ants can't do algebra. But that shouldn't be a surprise. Humans do all kinds of things animals can't. Plus, even humans weren't doing complex math until recently. The human species has been around for over three hundred thousand years. But it was less than 1,400 years ago that zero found its way into our number system.

Math is a cool and complicated subject. It's the science of space and quantity with all its related symbols. We can send rockets into outer space with math. But we also use it to do everyday activities. You might double a recipe when baking cookies. Or keep track of the scores and statistics for your favorite sports team. For most human cultures, it's as much a part of life as language. So where is the line between the math abilities of humans and those of animals?

After Clever Hans, many people thought animals couldn't do anything math-related. But the more scientists looked, the more they discovered. Abilities once thought to belong only to humans are shared with all kinds of animals. Think about the number sense of guppies. It's obvious they can make relative numerosity judgments just like people can. Not to mention, hyenas might be able to count. Parrots most certainly can. Plus, they understand number symbols. Chimpanzees can add and subtract. And honeybees understand zero better than really young children. So perhaps there isn't a dividing line between humans and animals at all. Maybe it's more about a range of abilities. And different animals, including humans, sit at different places within that range.

So, if we have number skills in common with animals, where did those skills come from? For example, we share a similar number sense with guppies. But we are land-dwelling mammals and guppies are fish. However, if you go back 450 million years, we share a common ancestor. It's possible we inherited our number sense from that creature. If it possessed a number sense, then it could have passed that along to the animals that evolved from it. And that ancestor led to more than just fish. We got amphibians, reptiles, birds, and mammals, including ourselves, too. All these groups display a number sense. So, it's possible we all inherited our skills from the same source.

But hold on! There is another possibility. Just because we all share a number sense doesn't mean it came from the same ancestor. After all, honeybees don't share that common guppy ancestor. Instead, we could have evolved our number abilities separately. That's known as **CONVERGENT EVOLUTION**. For example, birds and bats both have wings. But bats are

CONVERGENT EVOLUTION: when two or more species share a trait that has evolved independently

mammals. They didn't inherit their wings from a bird ancestor. They developed their wings for the same use as birds—to fly. But they evolved them on their own.

Perhaps guppies, hyenas, parrots, and people all had their own reasons for developing an understanding of numbers. And therefore, the same abilities evolved separately in each group. But for what reasons? It could be all about food. Knowing which patch of food is larger is a useful survival skill. Why waste your time and energy in the smaller patch? It could be about traveling through the environment. Learning to count landmarks, like honeybees do, can help you navigate. Or what about staying away from predators? Guppies choose the larger shoal to lower their chance of becoming lunch. It could be a good skill for predators, too. Comparing the size of your group to the size of the prey's group tells you the odds of a successful hunt.

Living in a social group would be another great reason to evolve number skills. The more group members to keep track of, the harder your brain needs to work. There is even more of a challenge if there is competition within your group for food or nest sites or mates. And what about defending your group's territory against neighboring groups? That's another reason to pay attention to numbers. Did you notice? All the animals in the previous chapters live in the wild in large social groups. Even honeybees, who don't share that common fish ancestor.

So, it's also possible we share number skills with animals thanks to convergent evolution. That's supported by the fact that all these groups have very different brains. The teeny brain of a honeybee is nothing like a large, wrinkly chimpanzee brain. But bees have a mental number line. All these different brains may have developed different ways to process numbers. And that's because each group had the same pressures to survive. So, just like the wings of bats and birds, different animals may have developed similar strategies. A sense of number or quantity allowed us all to stay alive.

A common ancestor or convergent evolution? Nobody knows for sure. For clues, we can look at living animals and compare what they can do. And there is still so much to learn. What else can animals do with numbers? Why do they do it? And where did those skills come from? Maybe some of these discoveries will be made by you.

ADD TO YOUR KNOWLEDGE

Introduction

AnimalWised. "(Clever Hans) The Horse That Learned Mathematics." YouTube, July 5, 2020. https://www.youtube.com/watch?v=hAJlAuEo7Ac.

"Clever Hans." Academic Kids. Accessed July 14, 2022. https://academickids.com/encyclopedia/index.php/Clever_Hans.

"Clever Hans Facts for Kids." Kiddle Encyclopedia. Accessed July 14, 2022. https://kids.kiddle.co/Clever_Hans.

Kokias, Kerri. *Clever Hans: The True Story of the Counting, Adding, and Time-Telling Horse*. New York: G. P. Putnam's Sons, 2020.

Rooney, Anne. *You Wouldn't Want to Live Without Math!* London: Franklin Watts, 2016.

Chapter 1: Fish Figures

Guppies Judge Group Size

"Are You Sensing Something?" Panamath Approximate Number System Test. Accessed July 15, 2022. https://panamath.org/index.php.

Laidlaw, Shawn. "Guppy." Biology Dictionary, September 7, 2020. https://biologydictionary.net/guppy/.

Sanders, Jessie. "Guppy Fish Species Profile." *The Spruce Pets*, December 10, 2021. https://www.thesprucepets.com/guppy-fish-species-profile-5078901.

Chapter 2: Counting Calls

Hyenas Tally Intruders

"Hyena." African Wildlife Foundation. Accessed July 15, 2022. https://www.awf.org/wildlife-conservation/hyena.

Marchant, Jo. "Hyenas Can Count Like Monkeys." *Nature*, August 17, 2011. https://www
    .nature.com/articles/news.2011.484.

Mononen, Riikka. "Counting Skills." iSeeNumbers. Accessed July 15, 2022. www
    .iseenumbers123.com/counting-skills.

"Spotted Hyena: *Crocuta crocuta*." San Diego Zoo. Accessed July 15, 2022. https://animals
    .sandiegozoo.org/animals/spotted-hyena.

"Why Do Hyenas Laugh?" *Smithsonian Magazine*. Accessed July 15, 2022. https://www
    .smithsonianmag.com/videos/category/science/why-do-hyenas-laugh/.

Chapter 3: Bird Brains

Alex the African Grey Parrot Uses Symbolic Numbers

AnimalWised. "The Smartest Parrot in the World." YouTube, July 26, 2020. https://www
    .youtube.com/watch?v=LJdrZ_34T1g.

Bradley, Jeremy. "How Arabic Numbers Were Invented." The Classroom. Accessed July 15,
    2022. https://www.theclassroom.com/arabic-numbers-were-invented-6959.html.

"Cardinal, Ordinal and Nominal Numbers." Math Is Fun. Accessed July 15, 2022. https://
    www.mathsisfun.com/numbers/cardinal-ordinal-nominal.html.

Holman, Rachel. "*Psittacus erithacus*." Animal Diversity Web. Accessed July 15, 2022. https://
    animaldiversity.org/accounts/Psittacus_erithacus/.

Spinner, Stephanie. *Alex the Parrot: No Ordinary Bird: A True Story*. New York: Alfred A. Knopf,
    2012.

Taylor, Ashley, P. "Why Do Parrots Talk?" *Audubon*, August 6, 2015. https://www.audubon
    .org/news/why-do-parrots-talk.

The Alex Foundation. Accessed July 15, 2022. https://alexfoundation.org/.

Chapter 4: Ape Addition

Chimpanzees Can Do Calculations

Brunette, Matt. "Do Chimpanzees Have Culture?" Jane Goodall Institute Canada, April 11,
    2018. https://janegoodall.ca/our-stories/do-chimpanzees-have-culture/.

"Chimpanzee: *Pan troglodytes*." San Diego Zoo. Accessed July 15, 2022. https://animals
.sandiegozoo.org/animals/chimpanzee.

Cohen-Brown, Brittany. "From Top to Bottom, Chimpanzee Social Hierarchy Is Amazing!" *Jane
Goodall's Good for All News*, July 10, 2018. https://news.janegoodall.org/2018/07/10
/top-bottom-chimpanzee-social-hierarchy-amazing/.

Goforth, Christine L. "Science Sunday: Field Research vs. Lab Research." The Dragonfly
Woman, February 26, 2012. https://thedragonflywoman.com/2012/02/26/field-vs-lab/.

Jane Goodall Institute USA. "Chimpanzee Tool Use." YouTube, October 28, 2016. https://
www.youtube.com/watch?v=KFbqeVXzra0.

McDonough, Roisin. "Chimpanzee Guide: Where They Live, What They Eat, and How They
Use Tools and Weapons." *Discover Wildlife*, July 13, 2022. https://www.discoverwildlife
.com/animal-facts/mammals/facts-about-chimpanzees/.

"*Pan troglodytes*: Chimpanzee." Animal Diversity Web. Accessed July 15, 2022. https://
animaldiversity.org/accounts/Pan_troglodytes/.

Chapter 5: Insect Integers

Honeybees Understand Zero

"10 Facts About Honey Bees!" National Geographic Kids. Accessed July 15, 2022. https://
www.natgeokids.com/uk/discover/animals/insects/honey-bees/.

Ball, Johnny. *Go Figure! A Totally Cool Book About Numbers*. New York: DK Publishing, 2005.

"Bee Waggle Dance." Ask a Biologist. Accessed August 10, 2022. https://askabiologist.asu
.edu/bee-dance-game/introduction.html.

"Bees Get (Eu)Social." Science World, June 3, 2015. https://www.scienceworld.ca/stories
/bees-get-eusocial/.

D'Agostino, Susan. "Secrets of Math from the Bee Whisperer." *Quanta Magazine*, January 22,
2020. https://www.quantamagazine.org/what-scarlett-howard-learns-from-the-bees-she
-teaches-20200122/.

Hammond, George, and Madison Blankenship. "*Apis mellifera*: Honey Bee." Animal Diversity
Web. Accessed July 15, 2022. https://animaldiversity.org/accounts/Apis_mellifera/.

Howard, Scarlett, Adrian Dyer, and Aurore Avarguès-Weber. "Bees Join an Elite Group of Species That Understands the Concept of Zero as a Number." *The Conversation*, June 7, 2018. https://theconversation.com/bees-join-an-elite-group-of-species-that-understands-the-concept-of-zero-as-a-number-97316.

McCallum, Ann. *The Secret Life of Math: Discover How (and Why) Numbers Have Survived from the Cave Dwellers to Us!* Nashville: Williamson Books, 2005.

Nickeson, Jaime, and Robert Wolfe. "Honeybees." NASA. Accessed July 15, 2022. https://honeybeenet.gsfc.nasa.gov/Honeybees/Basics.htm.

Resnick, Brian. "The Mind-Bendy Weirdness of the Number Zero, Explained." *Vox*, December 5, 2018. https://www.vox.com/science-and-health/2018/7/5/17500782/zero-number-math-explained.

Uyeno, Greg. "Here's All the Buzz About Honeybees." *Live Science*, November 13, 2020. https://www.livescience.com/honeybees.html.

"What's the Waggle Dance? And Why Do Honeybees Do It?" *Smithsonian Magazine*. Accessed July 15, 2022. https://www.smithsonianmag.com/videos/whats-the-waggle-dance-and-why-do-honeybees/.

Conclusion

2 Minute Classroom. "Convergent Evolution vs Divergent Evolution: Shared Traits Explained." YouTube, March 7, 2017. https://www.youtube.com/watch?v=X-XtZyHcck4.

Cepelewicz, Jordana. "Animals Count and Use Zero. How Far Does Their Number Sense Go?" *Quanta Magazine*, August 9, 2021. https://www.quantamagazine.org/animals-can-count-and-use-zero-how-far-does-their-number-sense-go-20210809/.

Milius, Susan. "Animals Can Do 'Almost Math.'" *Science News for Students*, December 12, 2016. www.sciencenewsforstudents.org/article/animals-can-do-almost-math.

Tennesen, Michael. "More Animals Seem to Have Some Ability to Count." *Scientific American*, September 1, 2009. https://www.scientificamerican.com/article/how-animals-have-the-ability-to-count/.

Wood, Charlie. "What Is Convergent Evolution?" *Live Science*, November 1, 2019. https://www.livescience.com/convergent-evolution.html.

BIBLIOGRAPHY

Agrillo, Christian, and Angelo Bisazza. "Understanding the Origin of Number Sense: A Review of Fish Studies." *Philosophical Transactions of the Royal Society B: Biological Sciences* 373, no. 1740 (February 2018): 20160511. http://doi.org/10.1098/rstb.2016.0511.

Agrillo, Christian, Laura Piffer, Angelo Bisazza, and Brian Butterworth. "Evidence for Two Numerical Systems That Are Similar in Humans and Guppies." *PLoS One* 7, no. 2 (February 2012): e31923. https://doi.org/10.1371/journal.pone.0031923.

Alberts, Elizabeth Claire. "This Is the Shocking Way Wild Parrots End Up as Pets." The Dodo, July 27, 2018. https://www.thedodo.com/in-the-wild/african-grey-parrot-pet-trade.

The Alex Foundation. Accessed July 15, 2022. https://alexfoundation.org/.

Avarguès-Weber, Aurore, Maria G. de Brito Sanchez, Martin Giurfa, and Adrian G. Dyer. "Aversive Reinforcement Improves Visual Discrimination Learning in Free-Flying Honeybees." *PLoS One* 5, no. 10: e15370. https://doi.org/10.1371/journal.pone.0015370.

"Bee Waggle Dance." Ask a Biologist. Accessed August 10, 2022. https://askabiologist.asu.edu/bee-dance-game/introduction.html.

Benson-Amram, Sarah, Geoff Gilfillan, and Karen McComb. "Numerical Assessment in the Wild: Insights from Social Carnivores." *Philosophical Transactions of the Royal Society B: Biological Sciences* 373, no. 1740 (2018): 20160508. https://doi.org/10.1098/rstb.2016.0508.

Benson-Amram, Sarah, Virginia K. Heinen, Sean L. Dryer, and Kay E. Holekamp. "Numerical Assessment and Individual Call Discrimination by Wild Spotted Hyaenas, *Crocuta crocuta*." *Animal Behaviour* 82, no. 4 (2011): 743–752. https://doi.org/10.1016/j.anbehav.2011.07.004.

Beran, M. "Proto-counting." In *Encyclopedia of Animal Cognition and Behavior*, edited by Jennifer Vonk and Todd Shackelford. Springer Cham, 2020. https://doi.org/10.1007/978-3-319-47829-6_728-1.

Biro, Dora, and Tetsuro Matsuzawa. "Use of Numerical Symbols by the Chimpanzee (*Pan troglodytes*): Cardinals, Ordinals, and the Introduction of Zero." *Animal Cognition* 4 (2001): 193–199. https://doi.org/10.1007/s100710100086.

Bisazza, Angelo, Laura Piffer, Giovanna Serena, and Christian Agrillo. "Ontogeny of Numerical Abilities in Fish." *PLoS One* 5, no. 11 (November 2010): e15516. https://doi.org/10.1371/journal.pone.0015516.

Black, Riley. "What Hyena Giggles Really Say." *National Geographic*, December 21, 2015. https://www.nationalgeographic.com/science/article/what-hyena-giggles-really-say.

Boysen, S. T. "Counting as the Chimpanzee Views It." In *Cognitive Aspects of Stimulus Control*, edited by W. K. Honig and J. Gregor Fetterman, 367–383. Hillsdale: Erlbaum, 1992.

———. "Counting in Chimpanzees: Nonhuman Principles and Emergent Properties of Number." In *The Development of Numerical Competence: Animal and Human Models*, edited by Sarah T. Boysen and E. John Capaldi, 39–59. Psychology Press, 1993.

Boysen, S. T., and Gary G. Berntson. "Numerical Competence in a Chimpanzee (*Pan troglodytes*)." *Journal of Comparative Psychology* 103, no.1 (1989): 23–31. https://doi.org/10.1037/0735-7036.103.1.23.

Butterworth, Brian, C. R. Gallistel, and Giorgio Vallortigara. "Introduction: The Origins of Numerical Abilities." *Philosophical Transactions of the Royal Society London B: Biological Sciences* 373, no. 1740 (February 2018): 20160507. https://doi.org/10.1098/rstb.2016.0507.

Cepelewicz, Jordana. "Animals Count and Use Zero. How Far Does Their Number Sense Go?" *Quanta Magazine*, August 9, 2021. https://www.quantamagazine.org/animals-can-count-and-use-zero-how-far-does-their-number-sense-go-20210809/.

"Chimpanzee: *Pan troglodytes*." San Diego Zoo. Accessed July 15, 2022. https://animals.sandiegozoo.org/animals/chimpanzee.

Chittka, Lars, and Karl Geiger. "Can Honey Bees Count Landmarks?" *Animal Behaviour* 49, no. 1 (January 1995): 159–164. https://doi.org/10.1016/0003-3472(95)80163-4.

Cohen-Brown, Brittany. "From Top to Bottom, Chimpanzee Social Hierarchy Is Amazing!" *Jane Goodall's Good for All News*, July 10, 2018. https://news.janegoodall.org/2018/07/10/top-bottom-chimpanzee-social-hierarchy-amazing/.

D'Agostino, Susan. "Secrets of Math from the Bee Whisperer." *Quanta Magazine*, January 22, 2020. https://www.quantamagazine.org/what-scarlett-howard-learns-from-the-bees-she-teaches-20200122/.

Dehaene, Stanislas. *The Number Sense: How the Mind Creates Mathematics*. New York: Oxford University Press, 2011.

Devlin, Keith. *The Math Gene: How Mathematical Thinking Evolved and Why Numbers Are Like Gossip*. New York: Basic Books, 2000.

Gatto, Elia, Olli J. Loukola, and Christian Agrillo. "Quantitative Abilities of Invertebrates: A Methodological Review." *Animal Cognition* 25 (July 2021): 5–19. https://doi.org/10.1007/s10071-021-01529-w.

Goforth, Christine L. "Science Sunday: Field Research vs. Lab Research." The Dragonfly Woman, February 26, 2012. https://thedragonflywoman.com/2012/02/26/field-vs-lab/.

Greenfieldboyce, Nell. "Math Bee: Honeybees Seem to Understand the Notion of Zero." NPR, June 7, 2018. https://www.npr.org/2018/06/07/617863467/math-bee-honeybees-seem-to-understand-the-notion-of-zero.

Hammond, George, and Madison Blankenship. "*Apis mellifera*: Honey Bee." Animal Diversity Web. Accessed July 15, 2022. https://animaldiversity.org/accounts/Apis_mellifera/.

Holman, Rachel. "*Psittacus erithacus*: Grey Parrot." Animal Diversity Web. Accessed July 15, 2022. https://animaldiversity.org/accounts/Psittacus_erithacus/.

Howard, Scarlett, Adrian Dyer, and Aurore Avarguès-Weber. "Bees Join an Elite Group of Species That Understands the Concept of Zero as a Number." *The Conversation*, June 7, 2018. https://theconversation.com/bees-join-an-elite-group-of-species-that-understands-the-concept-of-zero-as-a-number-97316.

Howard, Scarlett, Aurore Avargues-Weber, Jair E. Garcia, Andrew D. Greentree, and Adrian G. Dyer. "Numerical Cognition in Honeybees Enables Addition and Subtraction." *Science Advances* 5, no. 2 (February 2019): eaav0961. https://doi.org/10.1126/sciadv.aav0961.

———. "Numerical Ordering of Zero in Honeybees." *Science* 360, no. 6393 (June 2018): 1124–1126. https://doi.org/10.1126/science.aar497.

———. "Surpassing the Subitizing Threshold: Appetitive-Aversive Conditioning Improves Discrimination of Numerosities in Honeybees." *Journal of Experimental Biology* 222, no. 19 (2019): jeb205658. https://doi.org/10.1242/jeb.205658.

Howard, Scarlett, Julian Greentree, Aurore Avarguès-Weber, Jair E. Garcia, Andrew D. Greentree, and Adrian G. Dyer. "Numerosity Categorization by Parity in an Insect and Simple Neural Network." *Frontiers in Ecology and Evolution* 10 (April 2022): 805385. https://doi.org/10.3389/fevo.2022.805385.

Howard, Scarlett, Jürgen Schramme, Jair E. Garcia, Leslie Ng, Aurore Avarguès-Weber, Andrew D. Greentree, and Adrian G. Dyer. "Spontaneous Quantity Discrimination of Artificial Flowers by Foraging Honeybees." *Journal of Experimental Biology* 223, no. 9 (2020): jeb223610. https://doi.org/10.1242/jeb.223610.

Hyde, D. C. "Two Systems of Non-Symbolic Numerical Cognition." *Frontiers in Human Neuroscience* 5 (November 2011): 150. https://doi.org/10.3389/fnhum.2011.00150.

"Hyena." African Wildlife Foundation. Accessed July 15, 2022. https://www.awf.org/wildlife-conservation/hyena.

Irie, N., Mariko Hiraiwa-Hasegawa, and Nobuyuki Kutsukake. "Unique Numerical Competence of Asian Elephants on the Relative Numerosity Judgment Task." *Journal of Ethology* 37 (2019): 111–115. https://doi.org/10.1007/s10164-018-0563-y.

Katzin, Naama, Zahira Ziva Cohen, and Avashai Henik. "If It Looks, Sounds, or Feels Like Subitizing, Is It Subitizing? A Modulated Definition of Subitizing." *Psychonomic Bulletin & Review* 26 (2019): 790–797. https://doi.org/10.3758/s13423-018-1556-0.

Klump, Georg M., and H. Carl Gerhardt. "Mechanisms and Function of Call-Timing in Male-Male Interactions in Frogs." In *Playback and Studies of Animal Communication*, edited by P. K. McGregor, 153–174. Springer, 1992. https://doi.org/10.1007/978-1-4757-6203-7_11.

Laidlaw, Shawn. "Guppy." Biology Dictionary, September 7, 2020. https://biologydictionary.net/guppy/.

Law, Jason. "*Crocuta crocuta*: Spotted Hyena." Animal Diversity Web. Accessed July 14, 2022. https://animaldiversity.org/accounts/Crocuta_crocuta/.

Marchant, Jo. "Hyenas Can Count Like Monkeys." *Nature*, August 17, 2011. https://www.nature.com/articles/news.2011.484.

Marmasse, Natalia, Aggelos Bletsas, and Stefan Marti. "Numerical Mechanisms and Children's Concept of Numbers." The Media Laboratory, May 11, 2000. http://alumni.media.mit.edu/~stefanm/society/som_final.html.

Martin, Rowan O., Cristiana Sennia, and Neil C. D'Cruze. "Trade in Wild-Sourced African Grey Parrots: Insights via Social Media." *Global Ecology and Conservation* 15 (July 2018): 1–13. https://doi.org/10.1016/j.gecco.2018.e00429.

"Masai Mara National Park." Global Alliance of National Parks. Accessed August 7, 2022. https://national-parks.org/kenya/masai-mara.

McDonough, Roisin. "Chimpanzee Guide: Where They Live, What They Eat, and How They Use Tools and Weapons." *Discover Wildlife*, July 13, 2022. https://www.discoverwildlife.com/animal-facts/mammals/facts-about-chimpanzees/.

Miletto Petrazzini, Maria Elena. "Trained Quantity Abilities in Horses (*Equus caballus*): A Preliminary Investigation." *Behavioral Sciences* 4 (2014): 213–225. https://doi.org/10.3390/bs4030213.

Miletto Petrazzini, Maria Elena, Tyrone Lucon-Xiccato, Christian Agrillo, and Angelo Bisazza. "Use of Ordinal Information by Fish." *Scientific Reports* 5 (October 2015): 15497. https://doi.org/10.1038/srep15497.

Milius, Susan. "Animals Can Do 'Almost Math.'" *Science News for Students*, December 12, 2016. https://www.sciencenewsforstudents.org/article/animals-can-do-almost-math.

Nelson, Erik. "Studies Find a Connection Between Language Skills and Math in Animals." Global News, April 19, 2021. https://globalnews.ca/news/7003023/can-animals-talk/.

Newton-Fisher, Nicholas E. "The Hunting Behavior and Carnivory of Wild Chimpanzees." In *Handbook of Paleoanthropology*, edited by W. Henke and I. Tattersall, 1661–1691. Berlin: Springer, 2015. https://doi.org/10.1007/978-3-642-39979-4_42.

Nieder, Andreas. *A Brain for Numbers: The Biology of the Number Instinct.* Cambridge: The MIT Press, 2019.

———. "The Evolutionary History of Brains for Numbers." *Trends in Cognitive Sciences* 25, no. 7 (2021): 608–621. https://doi.org/10.1016/j.tics.2021.03.012.

———. "Representing Something Out of Nothing: The Dawning of Zero." *Trends in Cognitive Sciences* 20, no. 11 (2016): 830–842. https://doi.org/10.1016/j.tics.2016.08.008.

"*Pan troglodytes*: Chimpanzee." Animal Diversity Web. Accessed July 15, 2022. https://animaldiversity.org/accounts/Pan_troglodytes/.

Pepperberg, Irene M. *Alex & Me: How a Scientist and a Parrot Uncovered a Hidden World of Animal Intelligence—and Formed a Deep Bond in the Process.* New York: HarperCollins, 2008.

———. "Evidence for Conceptual Quantitative Abilities in the African Grey Parrot: Labeling of Cardinal Sets." *Ethology* 75, no. 1 (1987): 37–61. https://doi.org/10.1111/j.1439-0310.1987.tb00641.x.

———. "Further Evidence for Addition and Numerical Competence by a Grey Parrot (*Psittacus erithacus*)." *Animal Cognition* 15, no. 4 (2012): 711–717. https://doi.org/10.1007/s10071-012-0470-5.

———. "Grey Parrot (*Psittacus erithacus*) Numerical Abilities: Addition and Further Experiments on a Zero-Like Concept." *Journal of Comparative Psychology* 120, no. 1 (2006): 1–11. https://doi.org/10.1037/0735-7036.120.1.1.

———. "Numerical Competence in an African Gray Parrot (*Psittacus erithacus*)." *Journal of Comparative Psychology* 108, no. 1 (1994): 36–44. https://doi.org/10.1037/0735-7036.108.1.36.

———. "Ordinality and Inferential Abilities of a Grey Parrot (*Psittacus erithacus*)." *Journal of Comparative Psychology* 120, no. 3 (2006): 205–216. https://doi.org/10.1037/0735-7036.120.3.205.

Pepperberg, Irene M., and Susan Carey. "Grey Parrot Number Acquisition: The Inference of Cardinal Value from Ordinal Position on the Numeral List." *Cognition* 125, no. 2 (2012): 219–232. https://doi.org/10.1016/j.cognition.2012.07.003.

Pepperberg, Irene M., and Jesse D. Gordon. "Number Comprehension by a Grey Parrot (*Psittacus erithacus*), Including a Zero-Like Concept." *Journal of Comparative Psychology* 119, no. 2 (2005): 197–209. https://doi.org/10.1037/0735-7036.119.2.197.

Pfungst, Oskar. *Clever Hans (The Horse of Mr. Von Osten): A Contribution to Experimental Animal and Human Psychology*. New York: Henry Holt and Company, 1911.

Plotnik, Joshua M., Daniel L. Brubaker, Rachel Dale, Lydia N. Tiller, Hannah S. Mumby, and Nicola S. Clayton. "Elephants Have a Nose for Quantity." *Proceedings of the National Academy of Sciences* 116, no. 25 (2019): 12566–12571. https://doi.org/10.1073/pnas.1818284116.

"*Poecilia reticulata* (guppy)." Invasive Species Compendium. Accessed August 7, 2022. https://www.cabi.org/isc/datasheet/68208.

Resnick, Brian. "The Mind-Bendy Weirdness of the Number Zero, Explained." *Vox*, December 5, 2018. https://www.vox.com/science-and-health/2018/7/5/17500782/zero-number-math-explained.

Reznikova, Zhanna, and Boris Ryabko. "Numerical Competence in Animals, with an Insight from Ants." *Behaviour* 148, no. 4 (2011): 405–434. https://doi.org/10.1163/000579511X568562.

Rose, Gary J. "The Numerical Abilities of Anurans and Their Neural Correlates: Insights from Neuroethological Studies of Acoustic Communication." *Philosophical Transactions of the Royal Society B: Biological Sciences* 373, no. 1740 (February 2018): 20160512. https://doi.org/10.1098/rstb.2016.0512.

Samhita, Laasya, and Hans J. Gross. "The 'Clever Hans Phenomenon' Revisited." *Communicative & Integrative Biology* 6, no. 6 (November 2013): e27122. https://doi.org/10.4161/cib.27122.

Seghers, Benoni H. "Schooling Behavior in the Guppy (*Poecilia reticulata*): An Evolutionary Response to Predation." *Evolution* 28, no. 3 (September 1974): 486–489. https://doi.org/10.2307/2407174.

Silva, Shiroma, and Carl Miller. "Parrots for Sale: The Internet's Role in Illicit Trade." BBC News, February 5, 2022. https://www.bbc.com/news/technology-60247540.

Skorupski, Peter, HaDi MaBouDi, Hiruni Samadi Galpayage Dona, and Lars Chittka. "Counting Insects." *Philosophical Transactions of the Royal Society London B: Biological Sciences* 373, no. 1740 (February 2017): 20160513. https://doi.org/10.1098/rstb.2016.0513.

"Spotted Hyena: *Crocuta crocuta*." San Diego Zoo. Accessed July 15, 2022. https://animals.sandiegozoo.org/animals/spotted-hyena.

Springer. "Asian Elephants Could Be the Math Kings of the Jungle: Experimental Evidence Shows that Asian Elephants Possess Numerical Skills Similar to Those in Humans." ScienceDaily, October 2, 2018. www.sciencedaily.com/releases/2018/10/181022122856.htm.

Stanford, Craig, and Maddalena Bearzi. "A Bigger, Better Brain." *American Scientist* 98, no. 5 (October 2010): 402. https://www.americanscientist.org/article/a-bigger-better-brain.

Talk to the Animals. 2014. Season 1, episode 2. Directed by Kim Maddever. Aired July 17, 2014.

Taylor, Ashley, P. "Why Do Parrots Talk?" *Audubon*, August 6, 2015. https://www.audubon.org/news/why-do-parrots-talk.

Tennesen, Michael. "More Animals Seem to Have Some Ability to Count." *Scientific American*, September 1, 2009. https://www.scientificamerican.com/article/how-animals-have-the-ability-to-count/.

Theis, Kevin R., Keron M. Greene, Sarah R. Benson-Amram, and Kay E. Holekamp. "Sources of Variation in the Long-Distance Vocalizations of Spotted Hyenas." *Behaviour* 144, no. 5 (May 2007): 557–584. https://doi.org/10.1163/156853907780713046.

Theunissen, Frédéric, Steve Glickman, and Suzanne Page. "The Spotted Hyena Whoops, Giggles and Groans. What Do the Groans Mean?" Acoustics.org. Accessed August 10, 2022. https://acoustics.org/pressroom/httpdocs/155th/theunissen.htm.

"What's the Waggle Dance? And Why Do Honeybees Do It?" *Smithsonian Magazine*. Accessed July 15, 2022. https://www.smithsonianmag.com/videos/whats-the-waggle-dance-and-why-do-honeybees/.

Wood, Charlie. "What Is Convergent Evolution?" *Live Science*, November 1, 2019. https://www.livescience.com/convergent-evolution.html.

Woods, Robert. "Guppy Fish Care Guide & Species Profile." Fishkeeping World, January 21, 2022. https://www.fishkeepingworld.com/guppies.

ACKNOWLEDGMENTS

Sincere thanks to the animal scientists who generously gave their time for interviews, consultation, and fact-checking as well as provided photographs.

Fish Figures: Guppies Judge Group Size

Dr. Christian Agrillo, associate professor of psychology at the University of Padova

Counting Calls: Hyenas Tally Intruders

Dr. Sarah Benson-Amram, assistant professor of zoology at the University of British Columbia

Bird Brains: Alex the African Grey Parrot Uses Symbolic Numbers

Dr. Irene Pepperberg, comparative psychologist and president of The Alex Foundation

Ape Addition: Chimpanzees Can Do Calculations

Dr. Sarah Boysen, comparative psychologist (retired) from The Ohio State University

Insect Integers: Honeybees Understand Zero

Dr. Scarlett Howard, head of the Integrative Cognition, Ecology and Bio-inspiration Research Group at Monash University

I want to express my sincere gratitude to the editorial and design team at MIT Kids Press, an imprint of Candlewick Press, particularly Hilary Van Dusen for believing in and shaping my concept, Emily Stone and Jason Emmanuel for polishing my words, and Martha Kennedy and Rachel Wood for making the book look so engaging. Additional appreciation to Jaclyn Sinquett for her delightful illustrations. I would also like to thank my agent Jacqui Lipton, my critique partners, and my niece, Kyra, and nephew, Connor, for all their help with early drafts. Finally, a heartfelt thank you to my entire family for their endless support and patience with my animal and math trivia.

IMAGE CREDITS

INDEX

STEPHANIE GIBEAULT is a Canadian animal science expert with a master's in animal behavior and a bachelor's in ecology and evolution. She's been pooped on by monkeys, grumbled at by gorillas, and drooled on by dogs. Now she writes fiction and nonfiction books for children as well as articles for magazines and the internet. She does math puzzles to relax and lives just outside of Toronto.

JACLYN SINQUETT has illustrated many books for children, including *I Love Strawberries!* by Shannon Anderson and *Sincerely, Emerson* by Emerson Weber. She lives in New Jersey.